AN
UNSCHEDULED LIFE

JOSEPH HORGAN WORDS

BRIAN WHELAN PICTURES

AGENDA EDITIONS

ISBN 978–1–908527–07–3

First published in 2012 by Agenda Editions,
The Wheelwrights, Fletching Street,
Mayfield, East Sussex TN20 6TL

Printed and bound in Great Britain

Joseph Horgan was born in Birmingham of Irish immigrant parents. He has lived in Ireland since 1999. He is a poet, columnist, writer and reviewer. He has previously been shortlisted for a Hennessy Award for Irish Writing and in 2004 was the recipient of the Patrick Kavanagh Award for poetry. He is the author of two books, a poetry collection, *Slipping Letters Beneath the Sea* [Doghouse, 2008], and a prose work *The Song at Your Backdoor* [Collins Press, 2010]. His work has appeared on television and radio and his second book was chosen and serialised as an RTE 'Book on One'.

Brian Whelan was born in London of Irish immigrant parents. Since his training at The Royal Academy, he has felt compelled to paint from memory the city of his childhood from an East Anglian studio – depicting a sublime comedy of life's glories and tragedies on both religious and secular plains. His work has been acquired by St. Edmundsbury Cathedral, Suffolk, England; St Martins-in-the-Fields Church, Trafalgar Square, London; The Parador Dos Reis Catolicos, Santiago de Compostela, Spain; St Louis de Montfort Language School, Czestochowa, Poland; and CD covers for bands including The Popes with Shane MacGowan. Books featuring his work include: *Myth of Return; King Edmund – Saint and Martyr; London Irish Painting* and *The Exchange* and are available through www.brianwhelan.co.uk.

CONTENTS

Front cover painting: Newsvendor

Come down and let me in

There are still stars in the failing sky

My best kisses were there.
I hope you kept them.
I don't get up that early any more
to walk the waking streets and nod
at breadmen and milkmen,
watch weary nightshift workers
falling out of their skin,
like drunks,
passing shops
and the faint echo
of other countries.

I nicked a bottle from a doorstep for you,
put an elastic band around some daffodils
I couldn't believe,
there were still stars
in the failing sky.

Forget the politics of your body,
the other coloniser,
it's not a sin
there was a life
we couldn't get lost in.

Your best kisses.
I'm knocking on the door again.
Come down and let me in.

Beneath chimney stacks

There are places where we used to live

Past the Polish church on Paternoster Row
men are walking down the hill,

come home from empty work,
along neglected pavements,

beneath chimneys and stacks;
all the imaginary love affairs of fading men.

Summertime they return
to where older things happen,

stand in sky lit yards,
with dreams of leaving

and men walking down the hill
past the Polish church on Paternoster Row.

I have nothing to say to the city

Anchor

I have nothing to say to the city.
Silent
beneath it,
like a river.

It is the least I can do.
My tribute
of silence,
like prayer.

I am drunk beyond speech by the city.
Incoherent
and cowed,
like a child.

It is the least I can do.
My failure
of fitting,
like form.

I am emptied of words by the city.
Shifted
and tugged,
like air.

It is the least I can do.
My thinking
of broken,
like love.

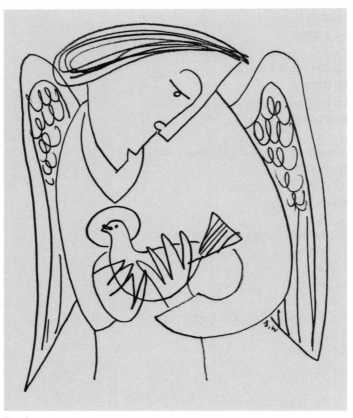

Loving care

Notices

People in the city die
in complete silence.
A notice appears overnight,
the details
of an unimagined life.
House numbers go into the hundreds,
As and Bs and Cs.
An address that does not exist.
In the loving care

of the long streets.
Passing away, again and again,
not many left by now
and in the end,
after all that,
their photographs come home.
A notice appears overnight.
People in the city die
near perfect deaths.

Songs that say…

Incomplete

We live there forever
in our own way,
after a fashion,
reduced
or is it enlarged
by songs that say this will last,
as if sound had mutated
into peripheral vision,
as we watch her beat her way through them
with truncheons and horses
as Orgreave plays over and over
and went out and drank at the lock-in,
our response,
listening to dying Luke and Billy and rebel songs
knowing revolution was just around the corner
and we were all Boys from the Blackstuff.
And then went to endless mass and college and were changed
even if we did not try to change and came back
to walk the streets we used to run as if we were now
Benny Profane coming home just for funerals and drinks
to a place where we couldn't exhale.
Our parents went home on the boat
while we went to all-nighters and dayers
and smoked and knew someone who could play the banjo
coming off shifts in London and Leeds and Birmingham
thinking the day we drank your bedding grant was the best day ever
to be listening to Shane on the jukebox.
That's the way the city is.
The human pattern.
We live there
in our own way,
after our fashion,
knowing it does not reduce us
in any way
just
makes us
forever.

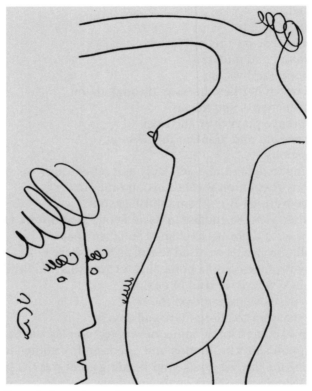

Love in botanic gardens

For the love of streets

In the northern city
I lift your dress.
There is a clamour beneath our skin.

We are still in love
in botanic gardens and snow
steeped streets and factory air
and rows and rows of red brick
steel mills
and the broken gantry
between the long convergence
of shattered warehouse windows.

Lives of quiet repetition fade
in the northern city.
Love passes over like a weather front.

Grounded

Handing out feminist tracts in the city centre

Her own, when they were women
did she think they should too
be so grateful
for such little slights
and ignorances,
such dissipated songs and postures
still kinetic and body married
into a chaos of being
should be swapped,
grounded,
by a fog of acceptance.

I saw you

I met my father in the street and we shook hands

I saw you in the distance, he said,
like the moon on a winter's day
or imagined planets breaking the horizon, I saw you,
on concrete by the fried chicken take-away,
past the used car corner sales,
like Jack Doyle on a wander, I saw you.

I'd recognise that swagger anywhere, he said,
and I swaggered and became
the day of a moon above the street
and unimagined planets rising
and the long, long city,
I saw you.

A generation of missing

The biography of Billy Mathews

Last known sighting?
What was he wearing?
Was there, by any chance, a forwarding address?
We'll have to wait
before we call this
a missing persons.
A generation of missing people.
This is Billy Mathews.

Did he swagger from the country?
Did he fall from the place?
Was he accompanied, at all?
A mother, a father, to see him off.
A sister? A brother?
Is there a likeness?
There isn't much to go on.
This, this, Billy Mathews.

Could there be a picture, say,
a Paddy in the Smoke,
dark suits, white shirts, modest
but moving, frenzied, outside
a city pub. The smell of tar.
Dropping in the milk, lifting up the latch,
the gears and the levers, singing, escaped.
This is Billy Mathews.

If he turned a Moss Side corner,
down a Small Heath street,
off at Archway listening,
the ever surprised sound of living
to be elsewhere.
I'm not saying you should forget too but I'd be sorry
to waste your time.
This is Billy Mathews.

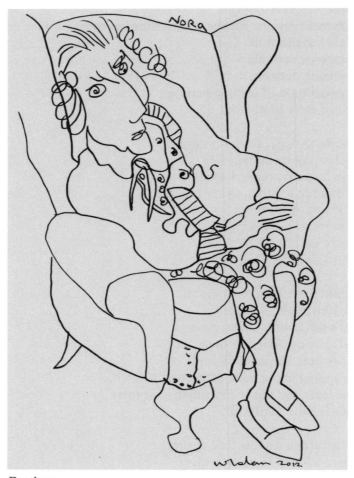

Restless

How irish women survived

I will not give up on this drawing of you, I said. And you said,
we both know, son, you cannot do it. And there is only a trace,
a scent, of cruelty in your words. After many years the city rose
in you, so that Irish cousins thought they might have an English
aunt. In truth, your voice paced back and forth. Not caged but
confused. Restless in both places. I believe I know what you look
like, I said. But I cannot draw you, if you will not sit still.

First Holy Communion

Growing up irish

Behind these streets lies another country.
With doors left slightly ajar our houses,
on Imperial Road or Lower Dartmouth Street,
never closed on a view of somewhere else.
Running away from the swish of First Holy Communion
to a metal slide and concrete interstices overlooked
by those bewildering clusters of high-rise flats.
As if the future had got lost.

Going home on the boat was an aberration.
We were to negotiate a different terrain
and coming back again was worse.
The tinge of dislocating regret
at returning to the city meant
we lost our footing.
In the end Ireland
cut the ground from underneath us.

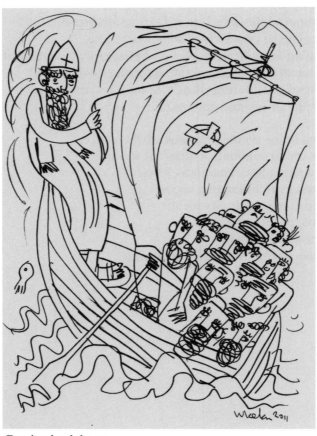

Coming back home

Holyhead

I only recognise
the strangers,
coming back home,
as they came home,
every sun-segued, rain-shaped summer,
lugging suitcases and trunks off the ferry
and better suits and dressed
than the set of clothes and Sunday best
they'd arrived in.
Home to a place that didn't exist.
Restless with the urge to run
they hid at the kitchen table,
on the street, in the pew, at the counter.
They couldn't breathe
for fresh air
and found
longing where they least expected it.

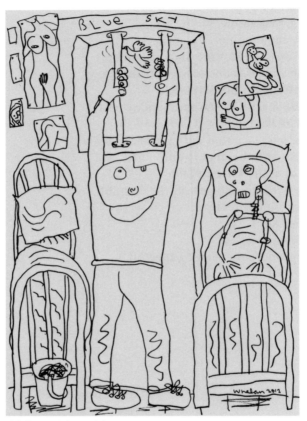

Giving a false address

Sound matter

Sound matter recorded
as if the city could be kept
so that lying awake anywhere
an ear tuned
to unhurried bus brakes
or bed-shaped sighs
and the still silence unmatched
of the four o'clock street;
you have been giving a false address
ever since.

An unscheduled life

The terminus

No pit stops
and banks and ditches
of found colour or forgotten grey.
No bypass exists.

As it was meant to be
this is corners and angles,
the unscheduled life,
it is valid

until the end of spring
and when seasons change
here comes sun, here comes rain.
It stops by request.

Join the queue,
wait in line
for public transport.

Clacking alarm

What that sounds like inside the city

Blackbird in the backyard,
of long forest tops,
of clacking alarm,
of endless anxiety and restless
nerve,
sings
of an evening
and the song sounds finest.
Yellow flags fly above the rooftops.

City centre

City centre

I have the old city in me and factories of the hand. I have smoke-fogged pubs at the end of corners. Corners of terraced houses. Shiftworkers still keep their own licence and the short walk home in the dark. I have the unofficial city in me and places only known to the city. A life on public transport is nothing to be ashamed of. I have the city in my lungs and I have had my moments. Keep on keeping on, I said. If it takes a year we're going to last a year. I have the city in my hands but I wouldn't glance at half this stuff you buy. This emporium of skin. Everything for sale, everything must go, everything has a price, everything, everything, everything. I have the city raining past me day after day and though I have no weather in here I have everything else. I have the city in here and the unofficial city and the city in my lungs and the city raining past me day after day after day.

Downhill bus

The city is us

You kept those flowers long past their shelf life.
These petrol bathed stalks will last forever, you said,
and as you mouthed I saw the pollen on my hands and heard
the bus come hurtling down the hill.

But I am returning the past to streets where it belongs.
Like a tabloid threat I have no use for,
those urban tremors follow me so much that we part
on nodding terms as I refuse to leave.

Those warming explosions of love

A private matter

This silent society,
a country, a fogbound airport;
for all our shouting on screen
a landscape
of private memories.
The faraway shifting of trains
and high walls topped with broken glass,
as if definition only exists
in the damp kitchens of the past.
Those warming explosions of love,
our love of expecting little.
In the new country there is no recognisable face.
A raised hand from a car,
putting a key to the front door.

Say small things often.
Shape silence
in order to break it.
We are who we are
when we put our colours on
and then we take them off again.
We wear our sponsors close to our heart.
Ah, go down to the yard,
a chisel;
in the disregarded air,
with no one looking,
we do our work.

Intersection

Intersection

Malik dances at the intersection
by rainbow lights and diurnal, nocturnal
floods of traffic moving through
interior rains and gutters overflowing.
They say he has a wife and kids.

Perhaps, in another life,
he loads up the people
carrier and takes them to sports,
parties and the Friday Mosque.
Do they know their dad
is such a good dancer?

Malik dances at the intersection,
a monsoon of movement.
The buses and the shopping trolley,
the taxis and the nights out
go past.
At the intersection Malik dances,
to music no one else can hear.

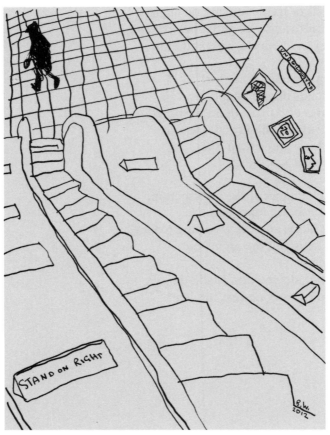

Under the starless streetlights

The unavoidable nature of fidelity

I curve my vowels around this place,
this brick on brick city,
this concrete lover,
inside my mouth,
around my tongue.
I speak of it wherever I go.
I give it
the fidelity of words.

Under the starless streetlights,
outlines and pencil drawings
of the lasting industry,
the interior factory.
I speak you and speak you and speak you.
Form on my lips.
An unbidden homage,
an unsought gift.

Digging their way back home

Nineteen seventy was a white new year

Nothing physical,
no scientific proof,
or reference book of records
but my brother-in-law's father
in a photograph of snow,
his black busman's coat and cap,
his black face against the white,
the low picket fence of our backyards
and I see my own immigrant father,
it must be the same year,
shovelling clear
the snow-built pavement outside our house
as I watch through the warm, wet window
his forward thrust and his backward lift
and the crumbling walls of snow behind him
though I can't see his face I can only see
the immigrant men driving, digging
their way back home.

My mind goes home

A note to Billy Mathews

The mind goes home,
like a pigeon,
like a tumbler
ricocheting through
invisible gradients,
to shit-smeared pigeon cages
and the imaginary city

where backyards are rooftops
and in the back of fag ash taxis
dulled and bruised, knowing too much,
there is enough
out and in, in and out of light, to realise,
like a tumbler, like a pigeon,
the mind goes home.

The widow

When the dancehalls closed

It wasn't those that stayed that built a country. It was those that left.
It wasn't the calling. It was the silence.
It wasn't the getting on a country bus. It was the boat.
It wasn't the unformed queue. It was the line.
It wasn't the perfidious. It was the faithful.

And if you are lucky, your way back with a shopping bag
along the streets, the widow or widowed,
the sideburned days and Sunday afternoon drinking gone;
a newspaper notice brings you home.
It wasn't the country. It was the city.

Flotsam and jetsam

The immigrant's self-portrait

See them floating,
the flotsam and the jetsam,
floating,
this country reared
for this,
this sin,
of being born

in that cottage,
on this lane,
to them,
they never leave,
this port or that
train station,
never leave
the point of departure,

never leave
floating
this city and that,
see them,
flotsam and jetsam
washing by,
floating.

When fathers were monsters

When fathers were monsters

In extreme circumstances people buy bread.
So when fathers were monsters
mothers took sons to the supermarket.
In silence.

Nothing lights up a yard like the moon.
By low-slung corrugated roofs you sit
and read the paper at midnight.
Plain Helvetica.

The city forgets everything under normal circumstances.
Daylight rises and bombers
become nothing but fathers.
For now.

Invisible

How irish women survived emigration

Being invisible had its advantages. Shunned on account of a
bombing, she found she could enjoy the silence. She no longer
had to make that kind of small talk. They put an extra bolt on
the front door.

In the summer she will be on a lane somewhere. High thorns
keep the fields from sight. A curlew calls like drumlin country.
Someone will come around a corner and ask. Are you home
from England?

Coming in from the lanes

Settling

Music in the walls and the taste
of meat cooking.
A conspiracy of lights and whispers.

A city only exists because we agree to it;
coming in from the lanes
we never knew what rain was in store.

And on a summer's evening with a phalanx
of badly-tuned children,
we leave streets of absence.

In transit we recommence laughing,
play at sleeping on the night boat.
Leave a key with the neighbours.

The waters of leaving

Last orders

The waters of leaving were black.
Nobody saw me.
I watched the prow cutting
sea like soil.
Leaving black ocean,
I never knew streets.
I left like the night.
A fox fled
and in the morning
I was gone.

Acknowledgements: Thanks to the editors of *Southword*, Cork, *Stony Thursday*, Limerick, *Poetry Salzburg Review*, Austria, and *Days of Roses*, London in which some of these poems have appeared.

Joseph Horgan wishes to acknowledge and thank the Arts Council of Ireland for their generous award of a bursary which contributed to the completion of this work.

Brian Whelan would like to thank Ron Rendell – a fellow traveller.